Four Pillars

**Building the Church
in an Age of Decline**

Four Pillars

Building the Church in an Age of Decline

David Cooke

Baptist House

baptisthouse.org

Unless otherwise noted, all Scripture taken from the New King James Version®. Copyright © 1982 by Thomas Nelson, Inc. Used by permission. All rights reserved.

Four Pillars:
Building the Church in an Age of Decline
Copyright © 2020 David T. E. S. Cooke

ISBN: 978-1-7774138-0-4

All rights reserved

Published by Baptist House
Woodstock, Ontario, Canada
baptisthouse.org

Cover Photograph by David Cooke
Church of St. Mary and the Martyrs
(Pantheon), Rome, 2018

SOLI DEO GLORIA

DEDICATION

To my father,
whose character, leadership, and wisdom
guide me in the Way.

ACKNOWLEDGEMENT

With deep gratitude to my wife for
proofreading and critiquing this book.

ACTS 2:40-47

And with many other words he testified and exhorted them, saying, "Be saved from this perverse generation."

Then those who gladly received his word were baptized; and that day about three thousand souls were added to them.

And they continued steadfastly in the apostles' doctrine and fellowship, in the breaking of bread, and in prayers.

Then fear came upon every soul, and many wonders and signs were done through the apostles.

Now all who believed were together, and had all things in common, and sold their possessions and goods, and divided them among all, as anyone had need.

So continuing daily with one accord in the temple, and breaking bread from house to house, they ate their food with gladness and simplicity of heart, praising God and having favour with all the people.

And the Lord added to the church daily those who were being saved.

CONTENTS

Introduction	13
A Bleeding Bride	17
The Power of Prayer	27
The Priority of Prayer	33
Dining with Jesus	47
A Word to Change the World	59
In It Together	71
Conclusion	85
Notes	89
Appendix	93
About the Author	97

INTRODUCTION

I love small town Ontario.

When my family left my childhood home in the suburbs of Toronto to move to the country, it was like we had travelled to another planet. The air was fresh, the pace was slow, and the drawl was long. Everyone knew everyone else's business – which was deeply disturbing at first, but oddly comforting over time. Neighbour helped neighbour. Strangers actually talked to each other in the grocery store and on the street. And at the core of our little community – both physically and spiritually – were seven busy, bustling churches.

That was over twenty years ago.

Last year (2019), my adopted home church, Walkerton Baptist, which was founded in 1879, shut its doors forever. Its historic building, strategically located opposite the old County Jail, has now been sold and converted into a multi-unit dwelling.

This year, two nearby sister churches also closed down. Beyond that, there have been countless other closures across rural Ontario in recent years. Meanwhile, many surviving churches are struggling and stressed.

I wish I could say this is only a small town phenomenon, but it is not. Unfortunately, we observe the same depressing trend multiplied in towns and cities all across North America. Churches are struggling, shrinking, and closing. As our culture becomes more post-modern and post-Christian, more people are looking at church as an archaic anachronism. Pressures are mounting from both within and without to change our tactics, shift our focus, and revise our values and beliefs.

With the arrival of a global pandemic, matters have only gotten worse. Where attendance was in decline before the coronavirus, it is now questionable if anyone will show up at all. Where offerings were low before, they have since bottomed out.

The church is experiencing enormous strain. There is pressure to adopt highly politicized health and safety protocols. There is pressure to conform to intrusive government regulations. There is pressure to endorse unbiblical cultural trends. And, finally, there is pressure to embrace a million-and-one church growth gimmicks that will supposedly heal all our ailments.

What is a church to do in these trying times?

There is only one answer: *the church needs to be the church*. It's just that simple. And that is precisely why I decided to write *Four Pillars*, a book based on a series of sermons I preached in several Ontario churches over the last decade.

Through a brief look at the early church as described in the Book of Acts, I want to help Christians see what the church truly *is*. Notice that I did not say "what the church *should be*". That is not the purpose of the Book of Acts. Acts is not some how-to guide. It is an historical account. The writer, Luke, gives us a picture of the sprouting New Testament church, recording facts and details in objective, news-report fashion.

When we look at the Book of Acts, we see what the early church *was*. By extension, and by comparison, we can recognize and embrace the marks of Christ's church today.

We will behold the *four essential pillars* that provide the structural integrity for this spiritual temple that our Lord is building. It is a design so wondrous and ingenious that the gates of hell will never prevail against it!

With that vision before our eyes, and with a renewed confidence in our Master Builder, it is my prayer that our worries for the future of the church will dissolve, and our hopes rebound, as we simply *be* the church – come what may.

A BLEEDING BRIDE

What if you came across a woman lying motionless on the side of the road? She is semi-conscious, and bleeding profusely. Her life is draining out of her. She's in real trouble. What do you do? Do you just think to yourself, 'It's not really my business,' and continue on your way? Or, maybe you stop for a moment, pull out a band-aid, put it on the wound, and move on. You pat yourself on the back and say, 'There. At least I did *something*. She'll be fine, I'm sure.' But is a band-aid good enough for someone bleeding to death? Or does that woman need some more serious intervention – some *intensive care?*

That woman is the Bride of Christ – the church. More specifically, it is the church as we find it in many places across North America in this twenty-first century. The church in the West is bleeding. It is like that woman on the side of the road, her life-blood pouring out of her.

With each new generation, fewer and fewer people are coming and staying. It is getting more difficult to keep our children. It is getting more difficult to reach the world around us.

The church in small town Ontario – my own home base – is just one example. Attendance is dwindling, priorities are shifting, doors are closing.

One church just north of Walkerton, named Paisley Baptist, boasted a membership of 310 souls. That was back in 1875. 133 years later (in 2008), when I spent a year there as pastor, they did well if they had a dozen people on a Sunday morning. As of 2020, they have permanently shut their doors. And it's the same story everywhere: churches are bleeding and dying. The Bride is fading fast!

How do we respond to this?

One option is to just continue on our way: simply ignore the problem and hope for the best. But we have seen where that leads – to another closed church.

A second option is to try a "band-aid" solution. A lot of churches use band-aids: 'fix up the building' is a popular one, jazz up the music, hold a potluck, do a fundraiser, run a programme.

As the father of two children, I know firsthand the relief that band-aids can bring. When kids get hurt, it's amazing how a simple band-aid can make them feel so much better. It might not actually help – but they *feel* better. And that's the problem with band-aid solutions: people *feel* better; but they don't get to the root of the problem.

What's needed, instead, is some radical intervention – some *intensive care*. That means getting back to God's plan and God's vision for His church. We need to see that vision and follow that plan once again, even as many churches saw it and followed it when they first opened their doors decades – or even centuries – ago.

The New Testament Church

In Acts chapter 2, we can trace the roots of the church back 2,000 years to the very first New Testament congregation – a group of about 120 believers. That is where it all started; that is where the vision is crystal clear.

When the festival of Pentecost arrived, thousands of Jewish people were gathered in Jerusalem to celebrate. That crowd saw God's Spirit at work in the 120 Christians, they heard Peter speak about Jesus, and their hearts were moved.

Then they ask Peter, "What shall we do?" In response, Peter answers them in v. 38: "Repent, and let every one of you be baptized in the name of Jesus Christ for the remission of sins; and you shall receive the gift of the Holy Spirit. For the promise is to you and to your children, and to all who are far off, as many as the Lord our God will call."

This is where the New Testament church really takes off. As we go on to read in v. 41, 3,000 souls respond to God's call and are added to the church that day.

This passage shows us the "doorway" into God's kingdom, the doorway into God's throne room, the doorway into God's church. And it is just the same doorway that we have today.

People still need to hear God's call and respond to His message by repenting and believing in Jesus. That's the *doorway*. Our mission as a church is to give the whole world every opportunity to come in through that doorway by sharing the Gospel far and wide.

The New Testament church took that mission very seriously. It didn't just stop on the day of Pentecost. It continued to spread the message.

Within only 300 years, the church had virtually taken over the Roman Empire – the most powerful civilization on the planet at that time.

Over the next 1,600 years, the church reached out across continents and oceans stretching out to the farthest, darkest corners of the globe. Over the last 2,000 years of history, every continent and country has been touched. There have been, literally, billions of souls enter into the church!

But how could the church achieve so much? What kept the church going and growing? How did it thrive down through the centuries, and how does it survive into our own darkening age?

Jesus tells us something very important about the church in Matthew 16:18. He says, "I will build My church; and the gates of hell shall not prevail against it."[1]

If we imagine the church as a great building – a temple – then the Lord Jesus is the Master Architect and Builder of that temple. It is His plan and vision, along with His ongoing supply of tools and materials, that is critical to our success. If *He* builds it, it cannot fail!

The doorway He has erected is *repentance and faith*. That is very clear. But, if we look inside the temple, we'll see that He has also established *four pillars* to keep it solid, strong, and stable. Just as long as these pillars are in place, the church will stand and that doorway will remain wide open. But without these pillars, there is no doorway, and there is no church.

The Four Pillars of the Church

After 3,000 new, Pentecost believers entered the doorway of the early church (as recorded in Acts 2:41), the very next verse brings us with them inside. And here is what we discover: "And they continued steadfastly in the apostles' doctrine and fellowship, in the breaking of bread, and in prayers."

These were the top four priorities of the infant church. These were the four concerns to which the earliest believers devoted their lives day-in and day-out, week-in and week-out. These are the four pillars of God's church.[2]

First Pillar: Apostles' Doctrine

The New Testament church was a learning church first and foremost. It was the seminary of the Holy Spirit with 3,000 pupils enrolled! Those believers were not just content to hear Peter's sermon and leave it at that. They wanted more. They felt in their souls a hunger for some meaty spiritual food – food that would feed, nourish, and grow them deep down inside.

They wanted to truly and deeply know this wonderful God and Saviour they had just met. This is why the Bible tells us they "continued steadfastly" – kept delving relentlessly and earnestly – into, first of all, the *apostles' doctrine*.

The apostles' doctrine is what we find in every page of sacred Scripture – recorded from Genesis to Revelation. Delivered by the hands of the prophets and apostles, the Bible is the Holy Spirit's textbook for the Holy Spirit's seminary.

Do you want to learn about God? Do you have a deep hunger in your soul for Him? Are you satisfying that hunger with the choicest food – feeding on the Word?

There are a lot of low-calorie substitutes out there – words of human philosophy and wisdom. Are you filling up on that empty fare? Or are you hearing God speak through His infallible Bible to every aspect of your life, your family, your job, your society?

Are you learning the wisdom of eternity, the mind of God, the plan of salvation, the truth of creation, the reality of heaven and hell? This is what the pillar of doctrine is all about – and it factored as priority number one in the early church.

Second Pillar: Fellowship

That word "fellowship", in spite of popular opinion, does not mean having a potluck dinner once a month. No. It speaks of a deeper relationship – a deeper bond. In fact, it is elsewhere translated "communion".[3]

In other words, the early Christians' lives were marked by a deep, meaningful, heartfelt relationship with one another. "They continued steadfastly in...fellowship".

They opened their hearts and homes, and shared their lives, their time, and their talents. They devoted themselves to the good of one another for the glory of Christ. If one brother needed help or support, the rest were there. They picked each other up when they were down. They bore each other's burdens. They got to know each other deeply. They held each other accountable. They cared like loving brothers and sisters *should* care.

How are we doing in the fellowship of the saints? How well do we *really* know one another?

Third Pillar: Breaking of Bread

The "breaking of bread" refers to that ordinance given by our Lord Jesus on the night before He died – the Lord's Supper. But the Lord's Supper isn't supposed to be a mere ritual – something we have to "get done" once a week or once a month. It is a special time to meet with our Lord; to dine with Him and celebrate what He has done for us at the cross.

This is what many theologians refer to as a "special means of grace". It is a special way that God has appointed for His people to experience His grace more fully and enter His presence more closely. This was a blessing that the New Testament church knew full well, and continued in steadfastly.

Fourth Pillar: Prayer

It is noteworthy that the word for prayer in Acts 2:42 is a *plural* in the original language. It reads "prayers".[4]

The New Testament church was a praying church. They used every type of prayer: private and secret prayers, family prayers, prayers during worship, prayers during fellowship, entire services of prayer. They continued earnestly in prayer. They prayed for themselves, prayed to intercede for the needs of others, prayed for their pastors, prayed for their rulers, prayed to give thanks, prayed to praise our Lord and Saviour.

Prayer is, simply put, "talking to God". It is not

some super-spiritual thing. When we talk to God, we are seeking His wisdom, unburdening our heart, asking for His help, and plugging into His will. These are some very powerful actions that produce some very powerful results.

Even prayers that are weak in faith, when earnestly and sincerely offered, are heard by God. He works through our prayers.

Keeping the Doorway Open

Thus, we have the four pillars of God's church: the apostles' doctrine, fellowship, the breaking of bread, and prayer.

No church can *truly* be a church without these four pillars. Chip away at one, and it's sure to get shaky. Damage two or more, and it is only a matter of time before it starts to collapse. The structure begins to crumble and the doorway gets blocked. New people stop coming. Old members complain.

Unfortunately, many churches today have lost sight of these four pillars. But without these pillars in place, you can't expect a church to grow. In fact, you don't even have a church!

Christ has shown us how He builds His church. He doesn't do it any other way. This is His plan – our Master Builder's blueprint.

THE POWER OF PRAYER

One of the most misunderstood and underappreciated pillars in the church today is the pillar of prayer. That is why I have chosen to start with prayer, and why I wrote two chapters to discuss it.

Prayer is not only absolutely vital to our churches, but it is absolutely vital to our individual lives. There is nothing like prayer to usher us into the very presence of the Almighty. There is nothing like prayer to open us up to His influence, direction, and will. There is nothing like prayer to help us realize our need for His power, and to help us tap into that power. And right now, no matter our situation, our heartache, our trouble, our need, our concern, our sickness, or our hurt, prayer will make an enormous difference.

The Bible says, "you do not have because you do not ask." (James 4:2).

Maybe you've heard the cliché "prayer changes things". Well, it's true. God uses our prayers to impact people and circumstances in ways we could never imagine.

Perhaps the most stunning example I could offer is a negative example: what happens when the pillar of prayer falls.

In 1962, the United States Supreme Court handed down a decision that would impact all of American society. That one ruling led to a total ban on all public prayer in government-funded schools.[5] Before that decision, prayer was part and parcel of school life for millions of students. But with one fatal blow, the pillar of prayer was axed.

What happened next is astounding.

Societal Decline

According to a 1990s landmark study[6] on social trends in the United States, a seismic shift took place right around the time when school prayer was banned. In every single statistic analyzed, the correlation between the removal of prayer and societal decline is unmistakable.

Whether we look at the numbers for teenage pregnancy, academic performance, youth suicide, or broader trends concerning crime, divorce, alcohol consumption, and beyond, we discover the same story. Society took a drastic turn for the worse once school prayer stopped.

For example, in the 1950s, the average violent crime rate had generally tracked with population growth. By 1962, around 250,000 violent crimes were committed every year in the United States. However, in the following decade, the crime rate nearly tripled, far surpassing population growth. Over the following decades, the upward trend continued. There were roughly 830,000 violent crimes in 1972, 1.3 million in 1982, and a peak of 1.9 million in 1992. That is 7½ times the 1962 average!

When we consider the rate of teen pregnancy, we see a similar pattern. Before 1962, there were about 15 babies born to every 1,000 unwed teenaged girls. After the ban on prayer, pregnancies tripled over the next three decades, rising to over 45 births per 1,000. With the rise in teen pregnancy also came a rise in abortion, only adding to this tragedy.[7]

Perhaps the grimmest statistic of all is the rate of youth suicide. It is truly alarming to see the change from the 1950s to the 1990s. Over this period, youth suicides increased by 300 per cent![8]

What do all these statistics show us? The implications are clear: if we take away prayer, things go downhill fast.

Prayer is powerful. We neglect this pillar at our peril.

When God Adds His Blessing

We have seen what happens when just one pillar is suddenly removed. The banishing of school prayer was a disaster. That was a fairly negative example.

What about a positive example? What happens when the pillar of prayer is firmly in place?

Let me share the experience of the New Testament church. After Luke reports that the early believers continued steadfastly in the apostles' doctrine, fellowship, the breaking of bread, and prayer, he writes in Acts 2:43: "Then fear came upon every soul, and many wonders and signs were done through the apostles." The power of God and the fear of God was manifest.

Then, in Acts 2:44 and 45 Luke describes how the believers shared their possessions and sacrificed to take care of one another: "Now all who believed were together, and had all things in common, and sold their possessions and goods, and divided them among all, as anyone had need." The family of God got closer.

Next, in Acts 2:46, Luke tells how the church would meet every day to worship God and learn together with joy: "So continuing daily with one accord in the temple, and breaking bread from house to house, they ate their food with gladness and simplicity of heart." It was a church plugged into God.

Lastly, in Acts 2:47, Luke reveals the one result we would simply love to see in our churches today. He writes: "And the Lord added to the church daily those who were being saved."

The pillars were strong, the "doorway" was wide open, and people were pouring in!

The Lord added His blessing to the New Testament church, and I believe He is willing and ready to do the same for us today. But we need to get back to God's vision and plan – what we find in the Book of Acts.

We need to remember that Jesus is the One who builds His church, and He has designed these four pillars to hold it up and keep it strong. If we take our eyes off these pillars, our churches will continue to bleed. They may even die. But if we really want a change, and if we are willing to try more than a band-aid solution, we must renew our focus and look to Christ's plan for His Body, His Bride. The church needs some intensive care.

THE PRIORITY OF PRAYER

In Acts chapter 12, we find the apostle Peter facing one of his most dire predicaments. Things looked awfully grim.

King Herod Agrippa was ruler over Jerusalem in those days. This particular Herod was the grandson of Herod the Great, the one who tried to have the new-born King Jesus killed in Bethlehem. Unfortunately, it seems Herod Agrippa had the same jealousy in his heart as his grandfather. He would tolerate no rivals. Thus, Luke records in Acts 12:1-3 how he persecuted the church, had the apostle James killed, and then went on to arrest Peter and throw him in jail.

Herod didn't take any chances. It was maximum security for Peter. There were four squads of four soldiers each assigned to keep watch, rotating day and night.

Normally, if there was an especially dangerous criminal in custody, that criminal would be locked away in a cell and chained to a Roman soldier twenty-four hours a day. But verse 6 shows just how paranoid Herod was about Peter. Peter was shackled not to one, but to *two* guards, and with *two* chains – one on each arm. Outside Peter's cell, the two other guards in the squad kept vigil.

The timing of all this was during the Passover festival. It appears that Herod was planning to have Peter executed just as soon as the festival was over. This would be a sort of a present to the Jewish leaders, who were also persecuting the early church. This was to be Peter's very last night on earth.

It all seemed so hopeless – not only for Peter, but for the whole church. There was simply no way out of this predicament, humanly speaking. Peter was done for; and with Peter killed, it'd be a real blow to the infant church. People must have been thinking it was curtains for those Christians! It must have looked like Christ's kingdom was about to crumble before mighty Herod's feet.

World vs. Church

In this situation – and countless others like it – the Bible reminds us that the church and the world are in a constant battle. Remember the words of Jesus, as He stood before Pontius Pilate, about to face the cross during a previous Passover festival. He said, "My kingdom is not of this world." (John

18:36).

Elsewhere we read: "For all that is in the world – the lust of the flesh, the lust of the eyes, and the pride of life – is not of the Father but is of the world." (1 John 2:16). "Do you not know that friendship with the world is enmity with God?" (James 4:4).

This world is in a war against God, His truth, and His righteousness. The people of this world, whether they know it or not (and most don't), are under Satan's power. They have been lulled into a moral and spiritual slumber, cradled in his death grip.

The church is fighting tooth and nail for every soul it can seize out of Satan's hand. As a result, we see some casualties: Christians get hurt or even worse. Just take a look at all the persecution believers face in our world today – in Nigeria, China, Iran, or even sometimes in our own country. Here, in Peter's situation, we have one very graphic example.

No amount of smarts is going to get Peter out. No amount of muscle is going to take down those guards. Even if the whole church took up arms (which the Lord had never commanded) it would be no match for the Roman army. It seemed truly hopeless.

However, there is one weapon that the church

could use. It's not a physical weapon like a sword or a gun, but it's something far more powerful.

It is the power of the powerless. The world can do nothing but flee and tremble before this force. The great army of Rome was no match against it.

It is the weapon of prayer.

Precepts for Prayer

The infant church understood the power of prayer, and they were quick to brandish this weapon in Peter's defence. In Acts 12:5, Luke records: "Peter was therefore kept in prison, but constant prayer was offered to God for him by the church." This one statement can tell us quite a lot about prayer.

First, notice *who* is praying. It's not just the pastors, not just the deacons, not just those really spiritually-gifted people in the congregation, not just the mid-week prayer group. It was *the whole church*. "The church" – all the believers – joined their hearts and voices together in prayer for the imprisoned apostle Peter. Each brother and sister had his and her part to play.

Do we understand the vital role each one of *us* plays in the battles the church faces today? Do we realize the critical importance of *our* prayers in the work of our local congregation, as well as the work of Christ's worldwide church militant? When we hear about some prayer need announced from the pulpit, or when we receive some news flash from a brother or sister, do we know just how serious it is? Do we understand how urgent it is that we get down on our knees and start praying? It is time to take up arms – to lift up arms – in prayer!

Second, notice *how* the church prayed. Verse 5 tells us that they prayed *constantly*. Another translation is *fervently*. Another, *earnestly*.[9]

This was prayer from the heart. They prayed with passion and conviction. They pleaded with the Lord, praying and praying and praying again for their beloved brother in chains.

They believed in the power of prayer. They knew that God hears prayer – that God sovereignly acts through our prayers. They understood that prayer literally changes our universe.

Do we have that same conviction and fervour in our own prayers? Do we pray from the heart? Or are our prayers a matter of habit – rote, cold, and stale?

Third, notice the object of the church's prayer in verse 5. They pray to *God*. This is an easy point to miss, but it's so important.

Hebrews 4:16 tells us, "Let us therefore come

boldly to the throne of grace, that we may obtain mercy and find grace to help in time of need." Because of the shed blood of Jesus Christ, not only do we have direct access to God in prayer, but we have the absolute assurance that He hears each and every prayer. The early Church knew that reality, and they were bold to take this hopeless situation directly to God.

Are we taking every situation we face – whether in our personal lives, in our society, or in the church – directly and boldly to the throne of grace? Are we going to God, or do we think we can handle things on our own?

The truth is revealed through our attitudes and actions. So often I try to reason out a solution in my own wisdom. I try to plan my way out of some predicament using my own ingenuity. I turn to my own resources *first*, when, really, it's pure folly.

After all, we have Almighty God on our side! We have the King of the universe in our court! How can we be so absurd as to not turn to Him in every matter first and foremost?

I remember when I served in a church in Port Colborne, Ontario. It was a little Baptist congregation with a dozen members. They met in an old building the Salvation Army had given up years before. They couldn't offer me too much in terms of pay – only $550 per month. My wife and

I were graciously allowed to use the back of the church as an apartment, which helped, but money was tight.

One day, when I went out for groceries, I stopped by the bank machine for cash. It was then that I discovered we only had $8 in our bank account. And since the machine only dispensed $20 bills, I had to return to our church home empty-handed.

I would like to think I was especially pious back then, with an unwavering faith in God's provision. But, to be honest, my very first thought was: 'What on earth am I going to do?!'

That was a truly foolish thing to think.

What I really needed to say, and what my wife and I started saying very earnestly and very quickly, was not 'what on earth are we going to do?' but 'what in heaven will You do, O Lord?'

The early church understood this. They prayed together – every believer was involved. They prayed fervently – with all their heart. They were bold to bring everything directly to God.

This is what a strong and powerful pillar of prayer looks like; and this is the model for our churches today.

Answered Prayer

In the battles we fight as the church, it often looks as though the world is winning. It often seems as though Satan is gaining ground. But we need to remember that looks can be deceiving.

The Lord has already told us which side is going to win. Jesus said, "be of good cheer, I have overcome the world." (John 16:33). That means it's a done deal!

The Lord Jesus is building His church, and the gates of hell shall not prevail against it. And the pillar of prayer stands as a pivotal part of His plan to win the victory.

In Acts 12:6, we continue with Peter chained in prison. The Passover festival was wrapping up, and Peter was about to face a speedy execution. It was, seemingly, the final hours of his life. Herod was planning to carry out Peter's sentence momentarily. Talk about hopeless!

But we need to see what can happen in that darkest, most hopeless moment – that "point of no return". Have you ever been in a situation like that? Maybe you are in that place right now – where all is lost, or so it seems! Financially, spiritually, health-wise, relationship-wise – we may be at the point of no return.

Behold what the Lord can do when the church prays!

In verse 7, as we find Peter sleeping, chained under heavy guard, we read: "Now behold, an angel of the Lord stood by him, and a light shone in the prison."

Amazing! The Lord chose this very moment – this "point of no return" – to show forth His power in the war against this world. He chose this darkest hour to shine his glorious light.

Thus, the angel wakes up Peter and raises him to his feet. His two chains fall off, and he is told to get dressed, put on his sandals, and follow. The angel takes Peter out past those two guards on either side of him, out of his cell, past the other two guards keeping watch, out the iron gate of the prison, and even down to the end of the street.

I don't know whether the guards were knocked out by the angel, or if God just froze time for Peter at that moment, but it was an awesome miracle. Peter was free! God answered the prayers of His church.

A Revealing Reaction

How the apostle reacted to this great deliverance is telling. In Acts 12:9, Luke writes: "[Peter] did not know that what was done by the angel was real, but thought he was seeing a vision."

I can totally understand Peter's response. If something like that happened to me, I'd have a hard time believing it was true. I'd have to pinch myself. And maybe that's what Peter does, because it takes him all the way to verse 11 – when he's down the street and the angel had left – for him to figure out what's going on.

What does that tell you about the strength of Peter's faith? Had he thought God would release him from prison? How high were his hopes for deliverance? Well, perhaps, not *so* high.

There is no doubt that Peter trusted in God. His faith in the reality of the resurrected Christ was unwavering. He also knew with certainty that His Lord Jesus would help him face Herod.

However, I suggest that Peter never imagined that God would actually set him free from prison! I am convinced that Peter was resolved to face the "inevitable" – death within a matter of hours, likely by crucifixion. But *should* he have resolved himself to this fate?

And what about us? Should we resolve ourselves to whatever may appear to be the "inevitables" in our own lives? Are we, perhaps, like Peter, being a wee bit pessimistic, or even presumptuous, by not believing that God really is able to do above and beyond all that we can ask or think?

After Peter pinches himself (at least metaphorically) and realizes he has been set free, he goes to bring word to the church. He remembers his brothers and sisters in the battle.

In verse 12, Luke reports: "So, when he had considered this [that God really had delivered him], he came to the house of Mary the mother of John whose surname was Mark, where many were gathered together praying."

It is extraordinary how the church was praying for Peter long into the night. But what is even more extraordinary is how God was answering their prayers at the very same time they were praying.

Then Peter starts knocking on the door. Knock, knock.

It is interesting how the believers react. Like Peter at first, they just can't believe it's true.

Sister Rhoda had gone to answer the door. Poor Rhoda. She gets such a bad rap. Do you ever notice how few parents name their daughters Rhoda? We think of her as some ditzy airhead. She goes to the door, hears Peter's voice, and then leaves him outside knocking while she goes back to tell the others. Come on, Rhoda!

But at least Rhoda actually believed it was Peter.

She was convinced. As for all the other prayer warriors, they thought she was raving mad. Only after some deliberation did they decide it must be some sort of angel – but it certainly couldn't be Peter! Meanwhile: knock, knock, knock.

Sometimes the church moves pretty slowly. *Sometimes* believers don't have all the faith they should when they pray. *Sometimes* their expectations aren't so high for what God can do. *Sometimes* they presume God will only act a certain way, but not another.

Nevertheless, God *can* and *will* do great and marvellous things when we pray. Don't ever *not* pray! Even if your prayers are feeble and weak, even if you don't know what to say or what to ask for. Don't ever *not* pray. Even if the "inevitable" seems absolutely inevitable, if you're discouraged – if the whole church is discouraged. Just pray and pray and pray with all your heart.

The Pillar of Prayer

God does some awesome things when His people pray. Psalm 50:15 sums it up when God Himself urges us: "Call upon Me in the day of trouble; I will deliver you, and you shall glorify Me."

That is exactly what happened in Peter's situation. In verse 17, after the believers finally opened the door and let him into the house, they were astonished. Then Peter led the church in giving the glory to God as he described his miraculous deliverance from the forces of this world.

It reminds me of that day when I was out of cash in Port Colborne – with only $8 in the bank. It was a dismal day. My wife and I needed to eat. We didn't know what to do. So, we prayed.

Just at that very moment, as we finished our prayer, a knock came at the back door of the church (where our apartment was located). A member of the congregation handed us an envelope with our name on it, and left without any ado.

We didn't know what it was about, and we certainly didn't expect anything miraculous. However, right there in that envelope, in immediate answer to our prayer, was $200 cash.

Needless to say, we did some mighty loud glorifying of God right then and there! We were able to get the groceries we needed; and we sure enjoyed our supper that night.

God is still at work today. He still delivers. The battle is His; not this world's.

That doesn't mean God does everything exactly

as we expect. That doesn't mean we will never be harmed or hurt. Peter would eventually be crucified years later, as history tells us,[10] called on by the Lord Jesus to testify to Him in death.

What we must always remember is that God doesn't always do what we *want*, but He always does what's *best*. And He chooses to use our prayers to do it.

The pillar of prayer is absolutely vital. It's an essential part of Christ's plan. It's critical to winning the battles before us. But if we want a strong pillar of prayer, we need to be praying. We need to pray together, with our brothers and sisters. We need to pray fervently and earnestly. We need to be bold in bringing every need directly to the throne of grace.

Remember: "you do not have because you do not ask." (James 4:2).

DINING WITH JESUS

The next pillar we turn to is the "breaking of bread", also known as the Lord's Supper. Some churches refer to this celebration as Communion or the Eucharist.

Two Ordinances

The Lord's Supper is an *ordinance* of the church. An ordinance is a practice specifically *ordained* by Christ for His people to observe again and again until He comes. Another word we use for this is *sacrament*.

Where *ordinance* puts the focus on *us* and what *we* have been ordered to do, *sacrament* puts the focus on *God* and what *He* does in and through these practices.

The Lord's Supper is not merely some human routine or ritual. It is appointed by God for His church, and God uses it to manifest His truth and grace.

How many ordinances are there? Is there more than the Lord's Supper? What about Baptism?

Roman Catholics claim there are seven sacraments: Baptism, Confirmation, Communion, Marriage, Confession, Ordination, and Last Rites. Most Protestants assert that the Bible only ordains two: Baptism and the Lord's Supper.

Nevertheless, Christians observe all kinds of different ceremonies: ordination and commissioning services, funerals, baby dedications, church dedications. Some anoint the sick with oil. Some practise foot-washing. Weddings are often the grandest of church celebrations.

However, when we consider what is *most* important to the calling and mission of the church, what is at the *very core* of its being, only two practices stand out. In terms of what Christ has ordained for believers to observe until He returns, only two are named. They are: Baptism and the Lord's Supper.[11]

That means anything and everything else must take second place in the church. Only two ceremonies deserve the place of highest honour and esteem among the people of God. And, yes, even weddings, with all their pomp and circumstance, must rank beneath these two!

First of all, Baptism marks our entrance into the

church. It's right there at the doorway. 'Repent, believe, and be baptized,' is how we follow Christ.

Baptism shows how God has washed away our sins, how He has raised us up from death to life in Jesus, how we have been born again. It is done *once* in a believer's life because it marks a *one-time* work of God in saving our souls and making us new. It is an occasion of great joy as the church joins with heaven in celebrating the salvation of a sinner.[12]

Second, there is the Lord's Supper. Throughout the Book of Acts, we hear it referred to as the "breaking of bread". Unlike Baptism, the Lord's Supper is not a one-time event in a believer's life. It is something every Christian needs to revisit again and again. The reasons for this, and for its exalted place in the life of the church, is the focus of the remainder of this chapter.

Communion at Troas

Most Americans know the name Buzz Aldrin. Buzz Aldrin and Neil Armstrong were the first two men to walk on the surface of the moon. What many may not realize is that Buzz Aldrin was an elder in his church.

When Aldrin went on his spaceflight to the moon, he took with him some bread and a cup. As soon as the craft landed safely on the lunar surface, he took that bread and cup and celebrated the Lord's Supper.

Why would Aldrin do this? Didn't he have more important things on his mind? Aldrin was about to be one of the first men to walk on the moon. He had just travelled on a 235,000 mile journey. Wasn't that awesome enough?

No. There was something more amazing to Aldrin. And it should be just as amazing to us, too. The Lord's Supper is critically important to the church; and it's critically important to the Lord of the church.

Paul understood the importance of the Lord's Supper. So did the church at Troas.

In Acts chapter 20, Luke describes a seven day stop-over the apostle Paul made in the city of Troas. This was during his missionary journey through Greece. It was Sunday – the Lord's Day, and verse 7 records that the believers had come together to celebrate the Lord's Supper and to hear a word from the apostle.

Luke writes: "when the disciples came together to break bread, Paul, ready to depart the next day, spoke to them and continued his message until midnight". Talk about a long sermon!

If we go back a few hundred years in history, we find that two- or three-hour sermons were not that uncommon in church. But even that is nothing compared to Paul's message in Troas.

Surprisingly, the saints in Troas didn't seem to mind one bit. In fact, they all stayed through the entire message (with one exception). To them, church wasn't just some religious duty or obligation. Church was their life.

The early Christians yearned to hear the great apostle opening up fresh insights for them from the Word of God. They were excited to hear what God had done in Paul's life. They were eager to hear of all the different places and people he had seen in his journeys, and all the different stories of souls touched, lives changed, and people won to Christ. This was awesome news. They were on the edge of their seats – and they didn't even have strobe lights or PowerPoint!

The believers sat and listened and talked, and the hours just flew by at light speed. At least they flew by for everyone except one young man named Eutychus.

Snoozing and Losing

There is a very common and troubling condition – a very serious affliction. It strikes all kinds of people, though, oddly enough, only when they're in church. Although most people *do* recover, especially if you give them a little nudge in the ribs, there are times when it is absolutely fatal. I call it "pew sleeper" syndrome.

As a preacher I've had far too much experience with this blight. The preacher can always spot the sleepers. But what's even worse than the sleepers are the *snorers*. Everyone knows who the snorers are. I remember trying to compete with a snorer once. I was preaching; he was snoring. The snorer won.

Eutychus was a sleeper. Verse 9 recounts the event: "And in a window sat a certain young man named Eutychus, who was sinking into a deep sleep. He was overcome by sleep; and as Paul continued speaking, he fell down from the third story and was taken up dead." This adds new meaning to the phrase 'you snooze, you lose.'

The first lesson, here, is this: when we come to church, we had better stay awake!

I love church. I get excited about church. Church is where we gather together to meet with God, to hear a message from His Word, to be with our brothers and sisters. But if we're dozing or groggy or just not fully with it, we're going to miss out. We need to be ready and alert and prepared for a blessing.

Eutychus would indeed meet with God at

church, but it would be in a very different way than he expected!

Despite what happened to Eutychus, I don't think we should be too hard on the lad. He was a young man, perhaps in his teens. Long sermons can try the attention span of even the oldest and wisest among us, let alone a teenage boy. Also, it was very late. With all those lamps burning for hours, the fumes probably didn't help. So Eutychus falls asleep – probably sitting on a window ledge – and falls three stories to his death. What a horrible thing to happen in a Sunday night service!

A Lord's Supper Miracle

As we read on, the night gets even more eventful. Luke writes in verse 10: "But Paul went down, fell on him, and embracing him said, 'Do not trouble yourselves, for his life is in him.'" Here we have recorded one of the great miracles of the Bible: Paul embraces Eutychus and his soul returns. The Lord raised this young man from the dead.

You might think Paul would call it a night after all this. But he doesn't. Notice what happens next.

Verse 11 tells us that Paul went back upstairs, broke bread, and continued preaching until *daybreak*. Now *that* is a long sermon!

When I first read this passage many years ago, it struck me as very strange. A young man dies in the middle of a church service, the pastor raises him from the dead, and then the believers go back and celebrate the Lord's Supper. Why would they do that? What is so special about this ordinance?

What Is the Lord's Supper?

There are five aspects to the Lord's Supper that reveal its immense importance. They show just how critical this pillar is to strengthen and build up Christ's church.

First, the Lord's Supper is about remembering the cross. As Jesus gave the bread and the cup to His disciples on the night before He died, He said, "Do this *in remembrance* of Me." Every element of the Supper has been ordained to direct our minds and hearts to Calvary. That is the very centre of God's plans and works and heart.

The bread that is broken reminds us of Christ's broken body, nailed to the cross. The cup that is poured out reminds us of the blood poured out as Jesus – the Lamb of God – was slain. We remember and ponder all the love and mercy of God at the cross. We look back through time 2,000 years and worship our crucified Saviour anew.

Second, the Lord's Supper is about God's love at the cross reaching out to us today. While we remember Christ's death as an historic event – something over and done with, its effects reach out far beyond the first century disciples.

When Jesus died, declaring, "It is finished," God unleashed a flood of grace and blessing on our world. That flood fills time and space, pours down through generations, and washes over believers from every tribe and tongue and nation. It is a flood that is still flowing today, which shall continue to flow unabated until the day when Christ returns.

This is why Jesus commands us to celebrate the Lord's Supper over and over. Every time we sit down before the table, Christ wants us to know that what He did on the cross 2,000 years ago was for you and me *today*. The love of the cross is here – yesterday, today, and forever – reaching out to all who will come. Those arms that were stretched out at Calvary are ready to embrace us even now.

Third, the Lord's Supper shows us how to receive the love of Christ *personally*. We remember the cross of history; we see how that cross reaches out to people today; but we still need to appropriate its blessings for ourselves. We need to take Jesus Christ as *our own* Saviour and God. We need to receive His embrace and accept His grace into our souls. We need to experience His cleansing and power in our lives *individually*.

How do we do that? As each one of us picks up that piece of bread and eats, as we take up that cup and drink, we are given a simple yet profound picture – a picture of faith. We're saying, 'I need You, Lord Jesus – Your broken body, Your shed blood. I trust in Your cross. I receive Your cleansing for My sins. I welcome You into my life.' That is what we need to do, each one of us. That is what saving faith is all about. And the Lord's Supper teaches us this.

Fourth, the Lord's Supper shows us how the cross of Christ is our source of blessing throughout life. As we come back time and again to the table, we see how, as believers, we need to keep coming back to Christ to provide for all our needs. We need to feed on Christ to strengthen our souls, to nourish our spirits, to grow in grace, maturity, and holiness.

When we come once again to the Supper, Christ shows us that we need to come once again to *Him*. In John chapter 6, Jesus said, "I am the living bread which came down from heaven. If anyone eats of this bread, he will live forever; and the bread that I shall give is My flesh, which I shall give for the life of the world... Whoever eats My flesh and drinks My blood has eternal life." (John 6:51,54).

Jesus is talking about how we need to feed on *Him*. He is describing how we need to be utterly dependent on Him for all our life, health, peace, safety, and salvation – every day. As we eat the bread and drink the cup at the Lord's Supper, it is a spiritual picture of feeding on the body and blood of Christ by faith.

Fifth and last, the Lord's Supper reveals the cross as our hope for the future. Because Jesus suffered for our sins and died as our sacrifice, we have a hope and a future. He took our place, which means His death was our death and His resurrection is our resurrection. We now enjoy eternal life in Him.

Therefore, when we come to the Lord's Supper, it is a little foretaste of that heavenly banquet we shall enjoy in eternity, seated with our King, the Lord Jesus. As we sit around the table, Jesus Himself is dining with us, celebrating His victory with us, and pointing us to the future.

It is no wonder that Paul, together with the church at Troas, celebrated the Lord's Supper after Eutychus was raised from the dead. They knew that it was Jesus' power and love that raised that dozing teenage boy. It was the power and love that God unleashed at the cross! And what better way to celebrate than to rejoice around the table, dining with their Lord?

Awake to the Lord's Supper

We all know it's true: 'you snooze, you lose.' But I'm not just talking about "pew sleeper" syndrome. When it comes to the Lord's Supper, if we are snoozing *spiritually*, we are going to miss out.

The Lord's Supper is vitally important. It is not some "add-on" we do at the end of the worship service. It is certainly not optional. And we have no right to change it. It is one of the pillars that Christ has designed to build up His church.

Are we clued in to what it means? Are we awake to what it reveals about the cross? Have we responded to its message? Are we giving this ordinance the rightful place it deserves in the church? Or are other things – other celebrations, events, and concerns – taking priority?

It may be wise to recall Paul's warning to those who would trivialize the Lord's Supper. He says, "For he who eats and drinks in an unworthy manner eats and drinks judgement to himself, not discerning the Lord's body. For this reason many are weak and sick among you, and many sleep." (1 Corinthians 11:29,30).

Let's wake up to the Lord's Supper!

A WORD TO CHANGE THE WORLD

In a survey conducted by Ligonier Ministries in 2020, American Christians were asked about their faith. The answers they gave are highly disturbing.[13]

Nearly half of respondents (49 per cent) said that Jesus is not God. 43 per cent said that the Bible is not literally true. 27 per cent claimed that science *disproves* the Bible. 19 per cent rejected the reality of hell. 31 per cent thought that abortion is *not* a sin. 34 per cent said that you can choose your own gender.

What is so very hard to fathom is that these are not atheists or agnostics responding, but self-declared Christians! If these professing believers are so out of touch with biblical truth, then is it any wonder that our society has become so pagan?

In 2007, Oxford University Press made some revisions to one of their main publications. In an effort to update the Oxford Junior Dictionary for today's young people, they decided to remove certain words that they deemed antiquated or archaic. Among the terms erased were "saint", "minister", "disciple", "sin", and "devil". The most current 2012 edition has continued this trend.

I don't know what world the publisher is living in, but it surely can't be this one! If they think the word "sin" is out of date for children, then I suspect they have no children of their own.

When my son was just two years old, he had a very distressing habit. Whenever we were in some public place, he would go up to all the little girls he could find and punch them. By age three, he graduated to body-slamming. Later on, he went through his steal-and-hide phase. Thankfully, he has since outgrown these habits that rather embarrassed his preacher-dad.

Like all of us, my children were born with a sinful nature – and they knew how to use it.[14] Our job, as parents, is to teach our kids not to follow that nature, and to find deliverance from it in Jesus. But, perhaps, it is not surprising that Oxford would cut words like "sin" and "devil" when we consider how many professing Christians are ignorant of the Scriptures.

The church, especially in the Western world,

has been greatly dumbed down. Believers know many of the basic words and phrases of Christianity, and some of the basic doctrines, but there is very little depth. There is very little understanding.

They don't have answers to tough questions. They don't have the knowledge and wisdom they need to navigate all the ups and downs of their daily lives. They don't know their Bibles.

When my home church, Walkerton Baptist, shut down in 2019, it was very upsetting. It surprised many people. But maybe it shouldn't have been a shock.

Just a few years prior, our local Christian bookstore closed. Around that time, when I was preaching at one of our sister churches, I said that this was a sign. It was a sign of what happens when the pillar of doctrine is neglected, and it portended some dark days ahead.

That Christian bookstore, which had been a community hub for decades, couldn't survive. Why? Was it because of online competition? Maybe in part. Or was it because Christians just weren't into studying, reading, and learning the Word like they used to be. Very likely. And as the pillar of doctrine totters and falls, churches totter and fall.

New Ground in Thessalonica

In Acts chapter 17, Luke gives us some insights into the apostle Paul's ministry. We see how the pillar of doctrine was constructed through Paul's preaching and teaching. This offers us the paradigm for Christ's church both then and now.

In verse 1, Luke records: "Now when they had passed through Amphipolis and Apollonia, they came to Thessalonica, where there was a synagogue of the Jews." The apostle Paul and Silas, after establishing a new church in Philippi, arrive in Thessalonica, the capital of Macedonia, a city of about 200,000 people.

Thessalonica was completely new ground for the Gospel. There were no Christians in this city, so Paul and Silas get to work planting a church right away.

Paul's first stop was the local Jewish synagogue, which he visited for three weeks. And what did he do there? Luke tells us: "Then Paul, as his custom was, went in to them, and for three Sabbaths reasoned with them from the Scriptures." (Acts 17:2).

Teaching the Bible is key to building a church. And we can follow Paul's teaching strategy in verses 2 and 3.

Relational Strategy

First of all, we see that Paul's strategy is *relational*. As a Jewish man and a renowned rabbi, Paul has an automatic "in" with any group of Jewish people anywhere. He can speak and relate to them as one Jew to another, and this is where he chooses to begin. Building on that *ethnic* and *cultural* relationship, he wants to develop a *spiritual* relationship in Christ. He opens up the Word of God to those closest to him first.

This is a good lesson for the church today. We need to build on relationships. We need to start with those we are connected with in some way already: family, friends, work colleagues, classmates, neighbours.

This is a good place to begin. We need to start shining the light of God's Word into the lives of those God has placed near us; then we move out from there.

Persistent Strategy

Besides having a *relational* strategy, Paul pursues a *persistent* strategy. For three Sabbaths he went to that synagogue in Thessalonica to open up the Scriptures. I'm sure that wasn't easy for him.

As Luke relates later on, some of the Jews were quite angry with his evangelism. Paul didn't receive the warmest reception. Nevertheless, Paul kept going back. He was persistent, determined, and patient. He planted the good seed, and he made sure to go back and water it several times.

This is another lesson for the church. We should never assume people are going to get it all the first time. When we open up God's Word with someone, even if we have a connection with that person, we've got to be prepared for misunderstanding, miscommunication, hesitation, or even outright rejection. But that should never deter us!

We need to go back to that person, explain things again in gentleness and love, clarify where needed, and pray that the Holy Spirit would do His work of opening the heart. God has given us the words of life; we need to do everything we can to share that life with others.

Even among the saints – our fellow believers – it is critical to be persistent in teaching God's Word. If the truth be told, we can be mighty ignorant and stubborn ourselves!

Isaiah 28:10 explains: "For precept must be upon precept, precept upon precept, line upon line, line upon line, here a little, there a little."

That is our teaching strategy. If we are going to grow strong in Christ, we need to get into His Word every day. We need to go over His Word again and again with one another. We need to build on what we already know – one step at a time, one relationship at a time.

Christ-Centred Strategy

As we have seen, Paul's approach to teaching is both *relational* and *persistent*. However, more importantly, it is *Christ-centred*. In everything he taught, Paul brought the focus onto Christ. At the end of verse 2, Luke tells us that Paul "reasoned with them from the Scriptures, explaining and demonstrating that the Christ had to suffer and rise again from the dead, and saying, 'This Jesus whom I preach to you is the Christ.'"

There are two components involved in Paul's Christ-centred strategy.

First, the apostle teaches how the Christ *must* suffer and rise again. In other words, Paul explains that the Messiah promised by God – the Christ presented throughout the Old Testament – is a figure who must suffer, die, and be raised from the dead. He must suffer the punishment for our sins, be crucified under the weight of God's curse, give up His life in our place, and then, on the third day, be resurrected to raise us to new life.

Perhaps Paul took his hearers to one of the

many prophecies of Christ in the Jewish Scriptures: Deuteronomy chapter 18, Psalms chapter 22, or Jeremiah chapter 23. Perhaps he took them to Isaiah chapter 53, which reads: "He was wounded for our transgressions, He was bruised for our iniquities; the chastisement for our peace was upon Him, and by His stripes we are healed." (Isaiah 53:5).

Whatever verses he quoted, Paul strove to demonstrate, first of all, that this was indeed God's plan from the beginning. This was what the Scriptures foretold, and this was at the heart of what the Jewish believers of old were expecting.

Second, after Paul showed what the Christ was to do and be, he goes on to prove that "this Jesus whom I preach to you is the Christ." In other words, he tells the story of Jesus – His birth, life, ministry, death, resurrection. He lines up everything Jesus did and said, and shows that this is the One – the Only One – who fulfills God's plan for Messiah. This Jesus alone is the One to whom all the Scriptures point.

Jesus Himself, in His own ministry on this earth, used the same strategy repeatedly. In Luke 9:22, Jesus told His followers, "The Son of Man must suffer many things, and be rejected by the elders and chief priests and scribes, and be killed, and be raised the third day." Then, after His resurrection, as He met with His disciples, Jesus said in Luke 24:46: "Thus it is written, and thus it was necessary for the Christ to suffer and to rise from the dead the third day."

The world needs to know *all* about Christ. People shouldn't just get a ten second sound-bite, or some slick slogan. We have to smarten up, and help others smarten up, too, when it comes to Jesus.

We need to understand the full-orbed plan of God for Christ to save us. We need to hear all about Christ in the Old Testament. We need to see everything Jesus did and said in the New Testament. We need to go deep into the work of the cross.

We need to grasp what it means for people today. We need to learn how it applies to broken homes and broken marriages, to raising children, to holding down a job, to running a country, to facing pain or persecution or a pandemic. We need to prepare for Christ's plans for this world in the days to come.

This is what the pillar of doctrine is all about. It is all about Christ, what He has done, and what He will do for us. No church will survive without a solid pillar of doctrine.

Divided Response

As we look, once again, at the ministry of Paul in Thessalonica, we observe the strategy he used: relational, persistent, Christ-centred teaching. He strove after a solid pillar of doctrine. As a result, we see a new doorway being opened into Christ's church in verse 4: "And some of them were persuaded; and a great multitude of the devout Greeks, and not a few of the leading women, joined Paul and Silas."

When the Word of God is taught, explained, expounded, and applied in depth, lives are changed. We should never underestimate what God will do through the power of His Word!

And yet, some churches hold back. Some churches are afraid. They know that what happens in verse 5 could happen to them, and they're scared.

Luke recounts in verse 5 that there were some Jews who were not persuaded by Paul. These Thessalonian unbelievers were enraged by the Gospel. They gathered a mob, attacked the place where the new believers likely met, and they brought some of the saints before the rulers of the city. It was quite a scene. The fledgling church was in real trouble.

Unfortunately, what happened back then in

Thessalonica is just as likely to happen today. The Gospel cuts two ways; and it can be scary.

Turning the World Upside Down

God's Word is a powerful weapon. It has the power to transform and the power to provoke. In verses 6 and 7, we hear the accusations hurled against the believers in Thessalonica. First, we're told that Paul and Silas "have turned the world upside down." Second, we hear that the Christians "are all acting contrary to the decrees of Caesar [the government authority], saying there is another king – Jesus."

This is a very perceptive statement. Though the Bible teaches us to love and honour all people, its message poses a real threat. It declares that we all have sinned – that this is a world of sin. Unless we believe in Jesus, it tells us that we will surely perish, along with this present world, when Jesus returns.

The Bible also talks about God's kingdom in terms of a foreign power. In fact, King Jesus is like a foreign invader seeking to take over this world and capture its citizens. All that is quite true, spiritually speaking.

Thus, many people feel threatened when we bring them the Gospel. They may even raise a ruckus when we intrude into their world. They may become enraged as we introduce a different set of rules and values, a different focus and perspective.

But that hostile reaction is nothing to fear. In fact, it's a good sign that we're doing our job right, and that God is going to change some lives, just as He did in Thessalonica.

In this day and age, when we see the dumbing down of the church, we need to respond by smartening up. The Bible says in 1 Timothy 3:15 that the church is "the pillar and ground of the truth." If we want our churches to be strong, to grow, and to turn our world upside down for Christ, then we need to make sure that the pillar of doctrine is solid and strong. We need to be sure that we are getting the Word *out* in a *relational, persistent,* and *Christ-centred* way. As we do, God will both change lives and challenge His people.

As the power of His Word is unleashed and the glory of His Word is exalted, the invasion begins.

IN IT TOGETHER

A survey was taken several years ago to examine the question of what makes a person choose a particular church.[15] Why do people pick one church over another? What are spiritual seekers really seeking?

Well, it's not cool tunes and free coffee.

It may be surprising to some that top of the list are "preaching" and "doctrine". Churchgoers want to be taught the Bible, which underlines just how critical the pillar of doctrine is.

However, next on the list is "friendliness". How the people of the church relate to one another makes a difference. This is where the pillar of fellowship comes into play.

Where there is good fellowship, the church is strong, and people from outside are drawn in. But where there is poor fellowship, the church is weak, and people are turned away.

Eating and Chatting?

What is *fellowship*, exactly? What is Christ's plan for this pillar? How do we "do" fellowship?

There are a lot of misconceptions out there when it comes to fellowship. One church I served in used to love "fellowship", or so they called it. They would always say, 'We should have another fellowship time.' However, what they meant by that was: Mrs. so-and-so should bake one of her famous pies, Mr. so-and-so should fire up the barbecue, and Miss so-and-so should make a salad.

There is this notion that fellowship means *food:* not necessarily a big potluck, but at least coffee and cookies. But is that what fellowship really means? Is it *eating?*

Others tend to think of fellowship in terms of *conversation.* To them, it means bringing folks from the church together to get to know each other better, to "catch up" on the latest news, to mesh and bond.

It's a *social* time – at least that's what many think. And if we just throw in a little reference to God – an ounce of spiritual content, we feel like we've had some real fellowship. But is that what fellowship means? Is it *chatting?*

Before I get in hot water, I just want to clarify that eating and chatting aren't bad things in and of themselves. However, true fellowship goes far beyond these. When we are suddenly faced with a pandemic, as we were in 2020, group meals and social gatherings are nixed, and the real state of our churches' pillar of fellowship is laid bare.

J. I. Packer, a renowned Canadian theologian, had this to say about our pre-pandemic practice of fellowship: "Christians today lack fellowship. We have many so-called 'fellowship' meetings, of different sorts, but the reality of fellowship is commonly absent, and, indeed, is rarely sought. That is because in our thinking we have substituted a secular, social idea of fellowship as a jolly get-together…We think we are enjoying fellowship when really we are not experiencing fellowship at all."[16] Those are some pretty tough words, but they are words we need to hear.

If we want to go deeper, if we want to really experience Christian fellowship, then we need to turn to the New Testament church. The very first believers had a passion for fellowship, and they can show us what it's all about.

Unity of Fellowship

Luke reports in Acts 4:32, "Now the multitude of those who believed were of one heart and one soul." Literally, in the original language, this passage can be translated: "the believers were heart and soul *one*."[17] There was a oneness deep down inside. There was a deep-rooted unity.

Our oneness in the church is a great concern to our Lord Jesus. He is not happy when His people are divided, disagreeing, putting each other down, working against each other. On the night before the cross, as He was about to face all the torture and pain of Calvary, at the forefront of Christ's mind was His people. He yearned for their unity in heart and soul.

It's really humbling to think that Jesus prayed for us in that dire moment. In John 17:20, Jesus says: "I do not pray for these alone [believers in the early church], but also for those who will believe in Me through their word [believers down through the generations]." And this is what Jesus asks for: "that they all may be one, as You, Father, are in Me, and I in You; that they also may be one in Us." (John 17:21). Then in verse 23, Jesus prays "that they may be made perfect in one," or as another translation puts it, that they may "be brought to complete unity."[18]

I believe that Christ knew this would be a big struggle for us, which is why He prayed so fervently. In response, the Father began to answer that prayer as the early church grew and spread; and He is still answering that prayer, today, where His people gather to seek His face.

There is a wonderful old hymn[19] that talks about the church's oneness in Christ. Its rich lyrics resonate in my heart every time I hear it:

> *Blest be the tie that binds*
> *Our hearts in Christian love;*
> *The fellowship of kindred minds*
> *Is like to that above.*
>
> *Before our Father's throne*
> *We pour our ardent prayers;*
> *Our fears, our hopes, our aims are one,*
> *Our comforts and our cares.*
>
> *When we asunder part,*
> *It gives us inward pain;*
> *But we shall still be joined in heart,*
> *And hope to meet again.*

True fellowship means being *one in heart*. It is having the same heart-felt, impassioned love for God. It is having the same heart-felt, sacrificial love for one another. It is having the same heart-felt yearning for God's kingdom to fill this earth, that the lost might be saved and brought into the joy of our fellowship.

It should pain us when we have to part, even if it's just for a week. It should grieve us that there are unbelievers outside the church who don't know the blessings we share inside.

True fellowship also means being *one in soul*. It is believing the same soul-saving truths. It is trusting in the same soul-transforming Gospel. It is sharing the same resolve and commitment deep-down inside to serve and glorify Christ. It is being determined together to reach this world for Jesus.

This is a oneness that reflects the oneness of heaven itself. It is the oneness and unity of true fellowship in Christ, joining in the purpose and passion of our Triune God.

However, we will never get to this point by merely breaking out the coffee and cookies. We need to work towards this oneness with the help of God, and it can take some very painstaking efforts. We need to get our hearts and souls on the same page. We need to have the same vision.

All Things In Common

The early believers experienced true fellowship. We see this in Acts chapter 4. They had a oneness at such a deep level that the fruits of their fellowship burst forth in some beautiful ways.

We see some of these fruits in verse 32: "Now the multitude of those who believed were of one heart and one soul; neither did anyone say that any of the things he possessed was his own, but they had all things in common."

The word for "in common" in the original language is the root word for "fellowship".[20] United in heart and soul, the believers opened up their hearts, lives, homes, and resources, sharing with one another. This is fellowship in action. This is what we yearn to see in the fellowship of the church today.

Down through history, there have been many people who have desired to create an ideal society. There have been countless philosophers, sociologists, and politicians who have sought to create a utopian community. They wanted a world where there is unity, where all are equal, and none are disadvantaged.

Karl Marx is one such example, with his philosophy of "communism", which he developed in the mid-1800s. Under the communist system, all the wealth of a nation is to be fairly and equitably redistributed. All property and possessions are held in common, private ownership is abolished, and social distinctions are erased.

Some, today, continue to insist that this is the best way forward. Communist redistribution is pitched as the progressive pathway to justice for all, counteracting inequalities in race, gender, and income.

Some have even turned to Scripture for their justification of communism,[21] citing verses like Acts 4:34. There, Luke reports: "Nor was there anyone among them who lacked; for all who were possessors of lands or houses sold them, and brought the proceeds of the things that were sold, and laid them at the apostles' feet; and they distributed to each as anyone had need." Doesn't that sound communist?

If we merely look at what the early Christians did, we might just miss the heart of the matter. If we only pay attention to the end results – that the church shared in everything, we will overlook how they got there. And how they got there is key.

The critical point is: no one was *forcing* anyone to give up anything in the early church. The apostle Peter and other leaders were not confiscating people's money and possessions. They were not forcibly redistributing believers' wealth to the needy according to some human plan. There is not even a hint of force or pressure.

The reality of what took place in the fellowship of the early church is the total opposite of the communist ideal. Individual believers were given the freedom to choose to share their own personal and private things to help each other. In that freedom, they gave willingly and gladly. It was a real work of God in people's hearts, guided and governed by Him.

When it comes to the pillar of fellowship today, nothing has changed. In God's wisdom and plan, true fellowship takes place when believers freely respond to God's prompting to help one another and share. Some give more, some less, as the Holy Spirit leads.

This is no cold, totalitarian scheme. This is no guilt trip. It is a movement driven by love and directed by God for His glory and praise.

All is God's

Fellowship begins with our oneness in heart and soul, being united in love, faith, and mission. From there it flows out in free and generous sharing. What drives it is not human force or obligation, but the Holy Spirit of God.

However, there is one more element that is

necessary to make this pillar strong. We need a *big* view of God and His kingdom. We need to recognize that our heavenly Father is the Almighty One, and He holds us all in His omnipotent hands.

In James 1:17, we read: "Every good gift and every perfect gift is from above, and comes down from the Father of lights, with whom there is no variation or shadow of turning." In other words, God has got His children covered, and that's never going to change!

But what does it mean, practically speaking, to have a big view of God?

It means I don't have to worry. I don't have to focus on the "trinity of self" (me, myself, and I). My Father loves me; He's in control. I don't have to be grasping or hoarding; God provides for His own.

So, why not give and sacrifice for others? Why not open up my heart to others? Why not allow God to use me to help some brother or sister? Why not share what God has given me? And why not allow others to share with me what God has given them?

John Calvin, a theologian and reformer from the 1500s, made a very apt observation as he studied Acts chapter 4. He said: "We must have hearts that are harder than iron if we are not moved by the reading of this narrative. In those days the believers gave abundantly of what was their own; we in our day are content not just jealously to retain what we possess, but callously to rob others... They sold their own possessions in those days; in our day it is the lust to purchase that reigns supreme."[22]

I think Calvin was right; and he is still right over 500 years later. So many churches today would be shocked at the idea of sharing like the early church shared. So many Christians are caught up in the materialism of this world; they're focused on looking out for "number one". But not only are they missing out on the joy of real fellowship; they are missing out on an opportunity to see the power and grace of the Almighty One at work in fresh new ways.

Power and Grace

In Acts 4:33, after writing about the wondrous fellowship of the early believers, Luke records: "And with great power the apostles gave witness to the resurrection of the Lord Jesus. And great grace was upon them all."

God's power and grace are unleashed beneath a strong pillar of fellowship. And that power and grace are not only felt by the brothers and sisters within the church, but the world outside takes notice as well.

When we witness to this world for Jesus, we don't just share the Gospel in word, but also in action. Often, when we think of actions that share Christ, we think of doing some good deed for a neighbour, showing forgiveness to an enemy, making a sacrifice for a stranger, contributing to some worthy cause.

However, one thing that we don't often think of is *fellowship*. The church's fellowship is a tremendous witness to this world. How we treat our brothers and sisters in Christ speaks volumes to a world full of scepticism and selfishness. As people *outside* hear about the fellowship we have *inside,* they will be drawn to us and, ultimately, to Jesus. Alternatively, when our fellowship is shallow, superficial, or insincere, not only will it hurt believers, it will turn off unbelievers.

When I look back over the years, I can see how many brothers and sisters demonstrated true fellowship in my own life and ministry.

For example, I fondly recall the time when I served as associate pastor at a predominantly Chinese Baptist church in Brampton, Ontario. I was overwhelmed by the fellowship I experienced as I took up my calling there in 2009.

When we moved into our home, dozens of

members came out to help us. They fixed up our new house and got us settled in without our asking. They painted our walls, de-weeded our lawn, and fixed a broken electrical outlet in my son's bedroom. They even remodelled our kitchen and babysat our kids – all without seeking anything in return.

There was such a sharing and giving spirit in that church. I will never forget it! In fact, shortly after we settled in, our next door neighbour told me that he had thought a Chinese family had moved into our house. There were so many church members helping us out, he assumed we were Chinese, too!

That is what true fellowship looks like. Where you find that oneness, that sharing and giving, that work of the Spirit, there the Gospel of Christ is on full display.

Example of Barnabas

Another example of fellowship in action comes to us at the very end of Acts chapter 4. It is a short account, but right to the point.

Luke records in verse 36: "And Joses, who was also named Barnabas by the apostles (which is translated Son of Encouragement), a Levite of the country of Cyprus, having land, sold it, and brought the money and laid it at the apostles' feet."

There was a need in the early church, and Barnabas was willing to meet that need by selling some of his property. He didn't have to make that sacrifice, but he wanted to; and it was a great encouragement to the believers. Now Barnabas is forever remembered for his gift. He is a model to us all of true fellowship.

A Place of Fellowship

Fellowship is more than eating and chatting. Those are fine things, but let's not get stuck there. You don't have to be a Christian to eat and chat. The pillar of fellowship is much bigger than that. Christ's plan for His church is much grander than that.

If we want to be a strong church, a welcoming church, a winsome church, we need to have a strong pillar of fellowship. We need to be a place of sharing and giving, united in heart and soul, one in love, faith, and mission. This is what Christ prayed for, and this is what He is building His church to be.

CONCLUSION

The apostles' doctrine. Fellowship. The breaking of bread. Prayer.

These are the four pillars of the church. Our Master Builder, the Lord Jesus, has designed and established these pillars as absolutely essential to the structural integrity of the spiritual temple that He is constructing. In every generation and in every location, these are the vital signs of the living, breathing, thriving Bride of Christ.

These four pillars are not commodities that churches need to acquire, or programmes they must implement. These pillars form the essence of what the true church *is*.

No pillars, no church. Only one pillar, no church. Two or three pillars, still no church.

Christ builds and strengthens His church by means of *all four* pillars. As long as they are in place, the doorway is wide open.

What does this mean during a pandemic, or in times of economic crisis, or amid persecution? Do Christ's plans change?

Not at all. Not one bit.

Regardless of our response to various outside forces, government edicts, or public health mandates, one thing is clear: these four pillars remain essential.

While Scripture commands us to be subject to the governing authorities (Romans 13:1), we also must remember that "we ought to obey God rather than men." (Acts 5:29). Therefore, we must be mindful never to work against the building plans of Christ, no matter the circumstances we face.

It is our calling, as Christians, to recognize what Christ is doing, submit ourselves to His plans, and get on board with His construction project. Then, and only then, will we find, as the believers in the Book of Acts found, that "the Lord added to the church daily those who were being saved." (Acts 2:47).

In these trying times full of enormous pressure on the church – from culture, government, and even from church growth gurus, let's take a fresh look at who we *are*.

Church, let's *be* the church!

NOTES

[1] King James Version.

[2] The Geneva Bible Notes from 1599 offer this perspective on Acts 2:42: "The marks of the true Church are the doctrine of the apostles, the duties of charity, the pure and simple administration of the ordinances, and the true invocation used by all of the faithful."

[3] The Greek New Testament word for "fellowship" is *koinonia*. It is also translated "communion" or "contribution".

[4] The Greek word for "prayer" in Acts 2:42 is *proseuchai*, which literally means "prayers".

[5] The Supreme Court decision in the Engel v. Vitale case resulted in a court-imposed ban on prayer in public schools in the United States in 1962.

[6] Statistics showing the decline of American society are taken from a study by Charles D. Barton: *America: to Pray? or Not to Pray?* (Wallbuilders, 1994).

[7] The abortion rate among pregnant teenage girls is 29 per cent, according to a Guttmacher Institute report: "Pregnancies, Births, and Abortions among Adolescents and Young Women in the United States, 2013" (2017).

[8] The 300 per cent youth suicide rate increase from the 1950s to the 1990s is highlighted in an article published by the American Academy of Pediatrics: *Pediatrics,* July 2016, 138 (1).

[9] The Greek word for "constantly" in Acts 12:5 is *ektenos*. It is also translated "fervently" or "earnestly".

[10] Eusebius of Caesarea recounts the crucifixion of the apostle Peter in his *Church History*.

[11] Christ ordains the practice of Baptism in Matthew 28:19 and Mark 16:16. He ordains the practice of the Lord's Supper in Matthew 26:26-28, Mark 14:22-24, and Luke 22:19,20. The apostle Paul also records the Lord's command for the Supper in 1 Corinthians 11:23-26.

[12] Jesus reveals the joy there is in heaven when sinners repent in Luke 15:7: "I say to you that likewise there will be more joy in heaven over one sinner who repents than over ninety-nine just persons who need no repentance."

[13] The complete findings of the 2020 Ligonier Ministries survey, entitled "The State of Theology", can be viewed on the internet at:

thestateoftheology.com

[14] The Bible reminds us of this obvious truth: "For all have sinned and fall short of the glory of God." (Romans 3:23).

[15] Survey data on why unchurched people choose a particular church are taken from a book by Thom S. Rainer: *Surprising Insights from the Unchurched and Proven Ways to Reach Them* (Zondervan, 2008).

[16] J.I. Packer provides an in-depth study of "fellowship" in his book entitled *18 Words: The Most Important Words You Will Ever Know* (Christian Focus, 2007), 191.

[17] A literal translation of Acts 4:32 from the Greek original is: "But of the multitude of those who believed, they were heart and soul one."

[18] New International Version.

[19] "Blest Be the Tie that Binds" was written by John Fawcett in 1782.

[20] The Greek word for "in common" in Acts 4:32 is *koina*, which is the root of the word *koinonia*, translated "fellowship."

[21] José Porfirio Miranda argues that "Christianity is communism" in his book entitled *Communism in the Bible* (Orbis Books, 1981).

[22] From John Calvin's *Commentary on the Acts of the Apostles* as quoted in John Stott, *The Message of Acts* (InterVarsity Press, 1994), 107.

APPENDIX

I leave you with this message from George Whitefield on the importance of *being* the church. Whitefield was a renowned evangelist, whose preaching led to the First Great Awakening in America. He delivered these words in 1740, at the close of his sermon on "The Necessity and Benefits of Religious Society."

Labour, therefore, my beloved brethren, to let your practice correspond to your profession: and think not that it will be sufficient for you to plead at the last day, "Lord have we not assembled ourselves together in Thy name, and enlivened each other, by singing psalms, and hymns, and spiritual songs?" For verily, I say unto you, notwithstanding this, our blessed Lord will bid you depart from Him; nay, you shall receive a greater damnation, if, in the midst of these great pretensions, you are found to be workers of iniquity.

But God forbid that any such evil should befall you; that there should be ever a Judas, ever a traitor, amongst such distinguished followers of our common Master. No, on the contrary, the excellency of your rules, the regularity of your meetings, and more especially your pious zeal in assembling in such a public and solemn manner so frequently in the year, persuade me to think that you are willing, not barely to seem, but to be in reality, Christians; and hope to be found at the last day, what you would be esteemed now, holy, sincere disciples of a crucified Redeemer.

Oh, may you always continue thus minded! And make it your daily, constant endeavour, both by precept and example, to turn all you converse with, more especially those of your own societies, in the same most blessed spirit and temper. Thus will you adorn the gospel of our Lord Jesus Christ in all things: thus will you anticipate the happiness of a future state; and by attending on, and improving the communion of saints on earth, make yourselves meet to join the communion and fellowship of the spirits of just men made perfect, of the holy angels, nay, of the ever-blessed and eternal God in heaven.

Which God of His infinite mercy grant through

Jesus Christ our Lord; to whom with the Father and the Holy Ghost, three persons and one God, be ascribed, as is most due, all honour and praise, might, majesty and dominion, now and forever. Amen.

Source: Evans Early American Imprint Collection: quod.lib.umich.edu/e/evans/N03788.0001.001

ABOUT THE AUTHOR

David Cooke graduated from Queen's University with a Bachelor of Arts, and from Toronto Baptist Seminary with a Master of Divinity. He served as a church pastor in Ontario, Canada, and as a missionary teacher in Honduras. He also directed CitizenGO Canada, a national non-profit organization defending Christian values in society. He presently serves with Campaign Life Coalition, and also does itinerant preaching and teaching. He is married and has two children.